An Old Leopard

POEMS BY LEANNA GASKINS

AN OLD LEOPARD (2015)

TRAINS AND COTTONWOOD SEEDS (2018)

An Old Leopard

Poems by

Leanna Gaskins

Vinland Books

San Francisco ● *London*

International Standard Book Number: 978-0-9907209-1-1

Library of Congress Control Number: 2015901499

First published 2015 by
Vinland Books
2443 Fillmore Street
San Francisco, CA 94115

Vinland Books
27, Old Gloucester Street
London WC1N 3XX

www.vinlandbooks.com

3 5 7 9 10 8 6 4 2

For Bob

When years ago we shuffled the words
To make the haiku,
What poem did we write among the electrons
That now speaks itself
In subtleties of days and roads?
The snow leopard, the peonies,
Bit by bit speak their names,
And shifting to and fro—
Zero and one, yin and yang—
Amaze every day the senses
With each new, bright harmony,
So softly and so perfectly they form.

Contents

AN OLD LEOPARD

I

An old leopard
With torn ears
Walks through the streets,
Amazed at each corner
By images not consonant with life,
Where no trace remains
Of what to hunt, or why.
Tired, seeking the solace
Of forest or glade,
But finding only
The long, barren slope
Of Kilimanjaro.

TIME AND SEASONS

II

Today there is a man by the door,
Painting permanently the number of the room
Upon the glass so long marked only
By black-crayoned, tentative figures
Scrawled in the corner.
And having stayed here in the building
Some years, settling into some kind of permanency,
No doubt accounts for firm black numbers
To mark the door and the pattern assured.
Yet spiders fill up the corners
With their own transient houses,
And changing days with vagrant dust
Mark the surfaces of living
With time's perpetual graffito.
It fills up the rooms with whispered silence,
Future unoccupancy swallowing even now
The footfalls of our passage.

III

That little girl in the photo,
Who is she?
Wind-teased hair and antique dress,
Spindly legs with great, knobby knees,
She squints into the sun,
Straining to see past its glare
The face of the old woman,
Who also squints from the shadows
And strains her gaze.
Their eyes can never meet—
A great blaze of sun-filled days
Stands taut between.

IV

Have we lived here for fifteen years?
For such a span of time to leave
So little trace of years or us
Seems but chicanery.
All the calendars and dates
Are but a jest of moving shells,
Deceptive and illusory.
"Now you see them, now you don't."
The mocking chant pervades these rooms.
Look here, the things we said we'd change
Are all the same, and show no mark
That fifteen changing years should scribe.
And yet it's true the walls bear cracks,
And here and there the paint looks dull,
Where sun and time have left a print.
Repeated footsteps wear a trail,
Though each be light as sun on silk.
So there they are, the years we've spent.
The evidence is clear enough.
Yet while we watched his other hand,
Old trickster Time has changed the shells.
And now invites us, "Bet again."
That years won't pass us by, unseen.

V

Sitting here in the hotel room,
In the sterile moments
Halfway between staying and going,
The eye is caught
By an edge of sheet come loose from the bed.
It's torn as by cat's claws.
Long, thin tears attest
To feline ferocity.
And there, perhaps a tooth mark
Beside the raveling edge.
One envisions the fierce little jaw,
The striped paws pulling and tugging,
Striving in vain to carry away
His oversized prey.
A frustrated swat and a hiss—
He disappears.

VI

It always seems to come too soon,
And always takes us by surprise,
The spring, emerging suddenly,
With trees aflower and gardens bright,
While winter lurks behind them all,
In shifting shadows of cold and rain,
To threaten all spring's hasty gifts.
But somehow, there, the season turns.
Between the evening and the morning,
Snow is exchanged for a world full of flowers.
It always seems to come too soon,
That look in the mirror, revealing the face
Of a parent we never thought to become.
Perception of autumn, coiled in the bones,
Long harvest of memories, carrying
The winter smell of empty fields.
It always seems to come too soon,
Before our arms grow strong enough
To carry what is now just ours,
Straining to learn how those before
Mastered the loads they bore until
Finally they stopped and set them down.

VII

Walking in the wind, I am reminded
Of all the years the wind has swirled away.
Of times and lives and shapes of ancient dreaming,
Folded like paper airplanes cast adrift
To navigate alone the soaring gale.
The track fades out behind like sandy footprints
That can't outlast the next incoming wave.
So, leaning into the wind, we stride on upward,
Till the wind in ceaseless change comes in behind
And pushes our footsteps faster along the trail.
Walking in the sun I am reminded
All times of dark and light alike converge
In sunlight and in silence on the mountain.
We climb these heights in darkness and sure hope,
To see the sunrise slant among the stones.

VIII

Standing by the mirror in the ending of the day,
I have seen the other images that join me where I stay.
The slant of sunlight fading across my bedroom wall
Reveals their subtle substance in pastel colors all,
The ones who stood at windows where I now briefly stand.
Knowing my presence passing, the shadow of my hand
That draws the curtains over to look across the way
At sunlight's lengthened shadows fading into gray.
The house is old and solemn and holds so many years.
They crowd among the sun's rays as evening now appears,
Surrounding me like fold on fold of gossamer array,
Displaying my own brevity in the ending of the day.

IX

There is no one now to carry us in,
For the years are past, and we are grown old.
And the days of sleeping in cold back seats
Are gone like the dreams of childhood times,
When everything was open and new,
And one could curl in the arms of sleep,
Knowing the strength of parents' love
Would come and lift us
And carry us in.
But now the battle is ours alone.
We fight sleep's urge and shiver in cold.
The strength that lifts us must now be ours,
For the arms that carried us are carried away.
Though the love lives on to warm the cold,
Until the angel who carries us home
Comes with the chariot warm as the sun,
There is no one now to carry us in.

X

Scraps of our living lie scattered all over,
Like leaves of the cottonwoods speckling the river.
If they were green once with promise of growing,
Somehow they withered almost without knowing
The glory of summer in sunlight and shower,
When blossoming seemed to be nearing each hour.
Yet time has no mercy on human or leaf.
The bright days of summer are golden and brief.
Now lengthening shadows lie cold on the lake,
And the wind from the mountains blows ice in its wake.
It scatters the remnants of every endeavor.
Faded and wan, they lie tossed on the river.

XI

Long, hard road, and no returning,
Never be what once I was.
That's OK, if from the burning,
I can rise like phoenix does.
Nothing much that I would cling to,
Little I would not let go,
If the creature I turn into
Meets the challenge that I know.
If the desert I am crossing
Burns away the dross in me,
I'll rejoice in every costing
That will buy my liberty.
Love, they say, is like a fire.
Well, if so, then let it burn.
Fuel it with my deep desire,
If its truth my ashes learn.

XII

Along the banks of this old river,
Many visions come and go.
The water flows along forever,
But for us it is not so.
Everything is passing, flowing,
On beyond our grasp to own,
And the river, ever changing,
Takes away what we have known.
In the shallows, it is easy
To imagine we can cross.
But the rapids soon inform us
Ventured easy, ventured lost.
And the river does not answer
To the pleas we might address.
All the waters flowing past us
Have their own unseen processes,
Their own channel flowing west.

CITY SCENES

XIII

Walking through the streets,
I heard the muzak playing.
Who knows from where?
The gas station on the corner?
The empty building where once
We came to send off holiday gifts?
Walking through the streets,
I heard the voices calling.
Who knows from where?
The grocery parking lot?
The playground on the hill,
Where families relax at close of day?
Walking through the streets,
I heard the silent whispers.
Who knows from where?
The times gather together,
And here among the shadows,
Along these changing streets,
They call and sing,
From who knows where.

XIV

I never thought to find a home
Among the city's restless streets.
For always to the mountain drawn,
In silence and in solitude
I thought to find my place.
But home is where you find it, and
In patient growth it builds its power.
Despite yourself, you are beguiled
And bound to love it from the hour
When faraway, you realize
That city block is calling you.
From mountain height or ocean shore,
The choice is made, you know it's true.

XV

Who lives in these houses, whose bright, lighted windows
We pass by in darkness and briefly see in?
A corner of mirror, an image of living,
A flash of wallpaper, a table and chairs.
Sometimes it's beguiling, warm-lighted and cozy,
A place one could sit and read by the fire.
But often so drab, dim and dull in the lamplight,
With spartan, bare walls, and curtains all frayed.
We muse how they live with so little of comfort.
These bright, empty rooms all set us to asking
What lives lived beyond us do they so enclose?
Ways we can't know, but only glimpse dimly,
In vaguely lit dramas of mysterious rooms.
And always the wall of the darkness conceals us
And leaves us to wonder,
And leaves them unknowing,
We passed through the night and asked who they are.
We look through their windows and go on our way,
Taking unfinished notions of who they could be.

XVI

Night and neon,
And here among the darkened streets,
An old leopard walks alone,
Seeing vague hints of knowledge
Reflected here and there.
Past silent windows,
Where, dim in the lamplight,
Companions converse of something,
Gone beyond the catching,
Even as their words emerge.
There at the corner,
Glimmers of peace and refuge.
But it's only the coffee house,
And the chairs by the firelight
Are full of tattooed children,
Seeking hope in cell phones.
Dim and fading,
Both the memory and the substance.
But still, through darkness,
Still, through flashing neon vapors,
Bound to the seeking,
The old leopard pursues
Some vision held and lost
Elsewhere on the other side of night.

XVII

Across the courtyard, darkened now,
I see your room in lamplight's glow.
Oh, neighbors, how it lights my heart
To see your home, you cannot know.
The pleasure of looking out at night
To see the homely scenes you share
Is such a comfort and delight
Just to know you living there.
Night by night and day by day,
The city makes it hard to know
Neighbors living side by side,
But when I see your window's glow,
It draws a bond of home and peace
To ease the heart with comfort too.
So I'll draw back my curtains so
And share my evening rooms with you.

OLD HOUSES

XVIII

That little, old house is empty now.
Outside its door the dumpster stands.
And all the memories collected there
Are gone into silence and other hands.
They held the sale a week ago.
Everything was there on show.
Now all that's left is a jumbled heap
Of trash and things no one cared to keep.
It's easy enough to stroll among
Possessions amassed by one unknown.
But then in the cold and silent dawn,
Forlorn discards somehow become
The link that ties all our lives in one,
With sorrow and pity for all that's gone.
It's soon enough the wreckers will come
For that sad, little house and its empty rooms.

XIX

Through the open door, the sunlight slants,
Dispelling all the vagueness of the hall,
Where dust has gathered softly in the corners,
And silence crowds behind the daylight's shoulder,
To see what might be passing in the street.
So many years are resident among
These aged walls and quiet-shrouded stairs.
In melancholy rose and palest gray,
Beside each curtained window, peering out,
The bygone times lift ribboned fans and sigh.
Somewhere chimes a clock, and languid light
Faints gracefully behind the closing door.

XX

Something about looking through a house,
Window to window and out again,
Is like looking through a tunnel's length
Into a place one has never been.
You know it's only someone's back yard,
The rear walls of houses, perhaps a tree.
Yet past all knowledge, a glamour falls.
They gleam like things that in dream we see.
Oh, if you stop and peer within,
The magic would fade, it's just a room.
So walk on by and keep the key
To that window gate on enchantment's home.

XXI

The pattern of the sunset light,
Shining through the curtain's lace,
Makes an image of the past
And draws the thought into that place.
The long ago when new this house
Stood among the new built roads,
And all the commerce of that age
By horse-drawn carriage brought the loads.
The street, the city are not old,
By standards of some other lands.
But still these houses hoard their years
And guard the gifts of many hands.
Among the sunset's changing hues,
These gentle shadows link us to
The solemn passage of the years
And all the glories that they knew.

XXII

Ah, the forlorn old house,
Loved and cherished so long.
But now other hands hold its life.
Its family and friends are all gone.
They tear out the walls and the doors.
They ruin the grandeur of age.
And replace it with plastic and cheap
Fad-inspired icons of change.
All of the history it holds
Is empty and shuttered to them.
And the beauty they blindly discard
Seems nothing but silly old trim.
Poor old house, you endured
So many years in this place.
How sad that your life is now lost,
Your beauty and strength all erased.

ROADS

XXIII

HIGHWAY 56, FORTY YEARS ON

The road here runs between green walls now,
Bounded by standing rows of tasseled corn.
King Wheat must share his throne.
And they're burning the wheat stubble,
Sending up great billows of smoke like funnel clouds,
With hot orange pickets of flame at their feet.
The fields are filled with awkward creatures—
Irrigation centipedes on vestigial legs,
Wind-tower dinosaurs flapping their flightless wings,
And oil-pump monkeys forever scratching their arm pits.
Yet the great land stretches familiar,
Broad fields framing old houses and older barns.
The landscape is dotted with small oases,
Where pioneers decided to make a homestead a home.
Though the road is full of trucks today,
Beside it, the railroad runs still.
Gaunt now with age,
And bereft alike of family, friends, and old enemies,
It confronts the new
With the patient gaze of an old settler
Living through one more drought.
This was always dark territory after all.

XXIV

They're naming the county roads now.
It seems the cities have won.
Those last vestiges of western prairie
Must soon slip away and be gone.
Sad loss those nameless little roads,
Always so beguiling in their anonymity,
Wandering away from highway and town,
Over a hill and into dream.
But now they have dull-sounding names—
Garden Lane and 110th Avenue—
To chain them to the cities' realm,
To tamed and ordered lands.
Ah, you can plant all the tallgrass you want,
Leave the tumbleweeds free to grow.
But when the last little road wears a name,
There'll be no wildness left to know.

XXV

Keep your eyes on the road.
Too many distractions allure.
Its track rises and falls
And curves blindly away,
Shrouded in mist, or glaring with sun,
The way still unwinds,
Endless to the horizon.
And many there are who travel blind,
Or, beguiled by some dream,
Turn aside and are lost.
Roads meet and part,
And connections, once lost,
Are not easily found.
One interchange here
May not interchange there.
Well, the circle comes back.
But that's a long way around.
Keep your eyes on the road.

XXVI

To walk down along that road again,
Dimly remembered track,
Footsteps slow in shade and sun,
Down to the creek and back.
The dusty ruts of an old dirt road,
Where no one ever came,
And one could walk in solitude,
With hate a distant name.
The trees were taller than a tree
Can ever hope to grow.
And peace and joy more tangible
Than ever more we'll know.
Fear confined to stories of
Creatures we never found.
Imagination building songs
Into every sound.
I know that road existed once,
But now I don't know where.
The years have built a precipice,
And I can't cross to there.

XXVII

I don't know what they're doing in Denver.
Today I can only look out
For what must be done here in the valley,
Down here where my life walks about.
What transpires in Denver still draws me.
I want to be there more than not.
But here is where time now deploys me.
The work I must do is the work that I've got.
Tomorrow, next week, perhaps leads me
Again to be walking in Denver, I know.
Today, though, there's my hallways for sweeping.
Today, this is my road, it's as far as I'll go.

XXVIII

It takes a long time, passing through
These little towns one does not know,
Until a day when something shifts,
And it becomes familiar now.
So every shop whose doors have closed
Is worth a sigh of sad regret.
And, sitting in a restaurant,
You think how much the times forget.
The grand old Main Street looks the same
As what it must have been when new.
But closer looks reveal the truth.
Those who come or care are few.
Oh, little Colorado towns,
There's meager good change brings to you.
May time relent and spare your grace,
To foster peace when we pass through.

XXIX

It's always a question of where you are
And what you can see from there.
For whether the road goes in or out
Depends on which side of the signs you read.
And whether the hill goes up or down
Is more a matter of where you look
Than slope or slant or altitude.
The complications of time and space
May make you forget that all things pass.
But turn the corner and look again.
The road's alright, it only takes
Adapting sight to fit the view
And measuring steps to stride on through.

PRAYER AND PRAISE

XXX

And the Kingdom of Heaven is like an old diner
That stood for a long time beside the road.
And they who passed by wrote it off and said,
Well, we'll get better food in the town.
But the children and the poor and hard-working
Came by there and saw
How inviting the cool and quiet interior,
With its comforting seats and respite
From the heat and dust of the way.
And so the lines grow long there,
Of folk who patiently wait,
To rest for a while among the gentle spaces,
Where the Spirit of God in humble service
Brings food and drink to those
Who hunger and thirst for righteousness.
And there by the road its old sign ever beckons,
Come unto Me, all ye who seek,
And I will give you rest.

XXXI

Will they ask us at the gateway
Whether we have read the words
Of the latest expert treatise
The defines the highest thinking
And expounds the brightest theories?
Will they tell us at the gateway
We're admitted if we know
All the key words of the doctrines,
All the scintillating structures
Of some unified field theory?
Will they chide us at the gateway
If we look a little doubtful
When we speak about the certain
Well-defined laws that we learned?
Will they turn us from the gateway
If we humbly say we don't know,
If we bow our heads in silence
And respectfully accept it
That our days were spent in labor,
But the harvest of our effort
Is a vapor that has vanished?
Will they then deny us entry?
Or will mercy recognize us
And accept our meager offering,
For the love that has sustained us
Till we came to this bright door,
Where our work can work no more.

XXXII

Sin has no share in being—
How true are the teacher's words.
But bitter its share in destruction,
Grievous its portion in darkness,
Wrought in the lives alike
Of sinner and victim of sin.
Who can perceive the dark malice,
The cruel deceit of its practice?
Framing its visage in glamor,
Blinding our eyes to reality,
Binding our lives to its travesty,
Till sudden the glare of the truth
Reveals the ruin and loss,
And hands the sinner the bill,
Demanding a payment in coin
No human hand can procure.
Oh, Lord of all creation,
You who alone are being,
If for nothing else we should worship,
For this, the great victory You won.
Forever, in the light of Your glory,
Sin must cower and wither,
Must stand unable to answer
And fade into nothing
Confronted with Being.
In whose bright Presence,
In whose true Being,
Sin can have no share.

XXXIII

Where was I when there was spoken
That bright word I long to hear?
Was I somewhere in the valley,
Seeking heights so far above me,
My strength could not bring me there?
Where was I when there came shining
That great light I long to see?
Was I sleeping in the forest,
Far below the shining summit,
Where the sunlight called for me?
Where was I when wind came rushing,
With the Spirit's flying wings?
Was I toiling under burdens
I should've long ago abandoned,
Bound by servitude to things?
Where was I when chains were broken,
And the bound rushed forth now free?
Lord, I hope that I was waiting.
Lord, I hope that I was ready,
When Your grace reached down for me.

XXXIV

Oh, kings of the earth,
Have you considered today?
He says He reproves
Even kings for the sake
Of the poor and the needy,
The helpless and lone.
For these, hear and ponder.
For these, kings and despots,
He will topple your throne.
Oh, kings of the earth,
Take heed to your ways.
Your power and weapons
Are helpless to save.
When you're called to make answer,
Alone you must stand.
No deed you committed,
No thought you imagined,
Can be hid from His hand.

XXXV

One by one, they pass before us,
All the visions of the years.
Try to understand the chorus
Of the songs they bring our ears.
Shall we ever again see them,
Those bright days now lost and gone?
Shall we walk again the pathways
We strode carelessly upon?
For we loved the things we saw then,
But we never understood
That beyond the day's cold ending,
All those things were gone for good.
Now we stand and face the crossroad.
Which way we shall choose to go.
Looking back, we wish for answers
From the life we used to know.
But in truth, the only signal
Is the one we see ahead.
We must hope it will be clearing.
We must pray it won't be red.

XXXVI

Sometimes it's like fire and brimstone,
Burning brighter than the sun.
And my strength cannot contain them,
All the words that would be born.
Feeble is my back to bear them,
For they multiply each day.
But my longing is for power—
To lift them higher on the way.
Sometimes it's like ice and silence,
Dragging downward in the night,
Dry and barren, lost and empty,
With no vestige left of sight.
In that darkness give me vision
Of the brightness that endures,
And the patience to outwait them,
In the knowledge that assures
All the shadows of the shallow,
All the glare of empty space,
Also will again be watered
With the Spirit's endless grace.

XXXVII

Bright blaze of sun fills all the room
And blinds the vision so
That all you see is flaming gold.
All else is lost in glow.
The eyes fill up with all this light,
And have no room to hold
Treasures beyond abundance vast
Of glory and of gold.
Across the roofs and battlements,
The power of sunlight flows.
Nothing can stand in its bright path,
Victor wherever it goes.
And ah, the spirit rises too,
Rejoicing in the light,
And sings while even its eyes are blind,
To stand somewhere so bright.

XXXVIII

The comic strip held words today
Of singular power and grace,
Endowed with wisdom seldom seen
In such unaccustomed place.
For there the child said to his father,
In words whose power grows,
Dad, I know only the riddle,
The answer I do not know.
And this the lesson we all need learn,
For all the ways we go,
The riddle surely we understand,
But the answer we do not know.
Oh Lord, You who know all the roads,
For Whom all ways are clear,
Grant vision to us faltering folk,
Who still are struggling here.
For Father, we also here must say,
We know the riddle too.
But for the answer we must stand
And wait the word from You.
For if we anything can claim,
The riddle's way to show,
Perhaps it's this to understand,
The answer we do not know.

XXXIX

Let me pass by unseen,
Too small for the dragon's gaze.
Turn away evil's eye,
All unaware of my ways.
Let all my steps be still,
Unheard by lurking foe.
Hidden from malice and ill,
In silence and peace to go.
Let dappled shadows fall
And camouflage my form,
My passage be unknown
To all who wish me harm.
Let wind arise and blend
My footprints with the dust,
That I may pass unseen
By all the rancorous.

XL

Set that down here, brother.
That looks too heavy
For us mere humans to carry.
Let me help you ease that.
Slip the straps and lay
That awful load down.
You were brave to lift it.
Don't let them tell you otherwise.
Don't let your mind either
Sell you short on courage.
Brother, you have borne it well,
Through all that hell-breathing
Terror of flame and darkness.
Set it down now.
For even our Lord once was weary
And stopped to set down his burden
At the Samaritan well.

XLI

While down the street in solitude
I passed at close of day,
I saw lace curtains blowing
In a window by the way.
And so entranced my vision,
To see their gentle sway,
I stopped and smiled in pleasure,
Before I went my way.
Is not this daily blessing,
To see the beauteous gift
Of everyday extravagance
That makes the spirit lift
And soar above mundanity
And every evil woe,
Crying glory to the God on high,
Who gives such gifts below.

LONDON DIARY

XLII

This morning's sun, with precise beam,
Picked out one leaf,
Transformed it into gleaming gold,
While yet the tree stood dim.
But now the fleeting sun is gone.
And here, in these familiar parks,
Autumn's province now,
Like amber drifts of snow,
The fallen leaves obscure the paths,
Unmarked by footfall of man or beast.
Above them all,
The ranks of trees stand faded and still.
But a row of lamps surprises,
With passing gleams among the dusky mists
Settling in windless calm.
So still the declining year
Rests after the revelry of summer.

XLIII

The Duchess

In Green Park always I see her,
The woman who walks with a limp.
Slender and upright, so the cane she carries
Seems almost an afterthought,
So swift and steady her pace.
She may be a bit older than I,
Her face marked by years in the sun.
But her white hair flies as she strides,
Carefree and bold in days of all kinds.
Her name I never have known,
But to me she is always the Duchess,
A lady of strength and distinction.
She looks a bit older these days—
It's been ten years after all.
But what can that matter?
Her bright, swift form remains
One of the potent images,
Like the ranks of great trees,
And the spring daffodils,
That define the character,
The enduring delight of Green Park.

XLIV

Those silly pigeons,
Always twirling in their mindless dances—
What mirage do they see,
That brings them to my windowsill?
Such a narrow space,
Its openness fenced by the empty brackets
That might have held bright oases
Of window boxes beckoning from the fourth storey.
An empty table too,
Its desert whiteness bone-dry and sere,
No faintest lingering wisp
Of grit-disguised breadcrumb or sunflower seed.
But they've been here again,
Since the rain last carried off their traces—
And left me an enigmatic token,
One pale gray feather, stuck to the glass.

XLV

Look there,
Daffodils crown the hill,
An ecstasy of gold in the morning light.
In ceaseless motion,
They bow amid the breezes,
To all the passers by.
Their pale green ankles flicker
Among their long, green skirts,
As they twirl and sway,
Flaunting their fancy frills
Beside the stern, gray grandeur of the trees.
Vivid upon their airy sweep of hill,
They dance through every moment
Of their brief, bright lives.

XLVI

She sits in the subway passage again,
Now that spring is here.
That Croatian woman—
Or Gypsy, or something—
Holds another baby on her lap.
Does she bear one every winter,
In order to sit so?
Whining, "Baay-bee, pleeease."
As she rattles small coins in her hand.
Graffiti grows everywhere,
No wall too hallowed to be marked on.
Even on the grand tree,
Opposite the duke's house,
Some oaf has scribbled an obscenity.
A neighbor chats of parking woes
And public incivility:
Trash littering the square
And dog droppings left on the footpaths.
Yes, and those homeless people—
One dressed in an expensive leather coat—
Tossing to the pigeons the remains of free food
The charities have provided them.
A bicycle careens past—
Up on the sidewalk again—
Just inches from her shoulder.
A shrug and a grimace,
"Ah, city living," she says.

XLVII

IMAGES

Among the last wan leaves of fall,
The crocuses appear.
And though the days are short and cold,
It surely seems
That spring is drawing near.

A squirrel digs beneath the trees,
Seeking a buried treat.
But stranger squirrels have planted here,
And flowers bloom,
Displacing food he'd eat.

The guardsmen at the palace gate,
Wearing winter gray,
Are drab among the daffodils.
But red soon comes,
To color drab away.

I saw the children playing there,
And not one wore
The gloves and scarves of yesterday,
These harbingers
Of springtime at the door.

XLVIII

MOVING AWAY

Wandering from room to room,
Feeling at loose ends—
Even a little lost—
In this space that was so long home.
The years all rush together and collide,
Scattering memories along the sun-dappled floors
And silence through all the rooms.
Leaving has been so busy till now,
Each day filled minute to minute,
With no moment left for regret.
Now these big, empty rooms
Echo to every whisper
And reach after our receding footsteps
With the sounds of our living,
To follow us down the stairs
And out into the years.

RAILROAD AND RIVER

XLIX

Little river towns,
Railroad towns,
You with the curious names—
Parachute and Rifle and Silt—
How will you live,
Now that the railroad mostly ignores you,
As the river always has?
Will you leave your beautiful valley,
Abandon your bright, fertile fields,
And the gorgeous, unknowable cliffs
That have always framed your sky?
Where could you go?
If the railroad deserts you,
Is there another haven?
How much easier the question
For those who live in cities,
Where the loss is only measured in dollars,
Not the long braiding of life with life,
And the railroad the only true power
Of motion upstream and down.

L

On a summer night, in a place long lost,
With moonlight white on the tracks and trains,
I boarded the cars of the Santa Fe
And left behind the life that remained.
West through the night, I abandoned youth,
Embracing the burdens unseen, unthought,
While, with faces still in the station's lights,
My parents stood with the farewell they brought.
And the train, that power of division and growth,
Silent, parted our lives, unaware.
Now, from the distance of years and dreams,
More clearly than daylight I see us there.
Now when nothing remains the same,
The station is closed; the trains don't run.
The Santa Fe itself is gone.
The parents too, long years done.
But yet the days stretch out for us,
Who try to learn the meaning of
The passing times,
The passing tracks,
And trains that never bear us back.

LI

Old river, you invade my dreams,
And leave me wondering when I wake,
How much of me has floated down
Your reaches into some dark lake.
Old river, not too long ago,
I passed you by in hurried run,
Until one day I chanced to stop,
And walked beside you in the sun.
Your spell, old river, captivates.
It isn't obvious at first,
But soon the mind reverberates
To your dark ripples and the thirst
To walk again along your banks,
Where ever flowing waters cold
Grow behind the dam of years,
And soon our thoughts and dreams enfold.

LII

Down there by the water,
Where they built the new ballpark,
Where the gleaming highrises—
Thirty floors of luxury—
Rise in the shadows
Of the Bay Bridge approaches.
Among the bright shop fronts,
The stores and the promenades,
Look there, by the palm trees,
Right past that last tour bus,
Ghost trains of the Belt Line,
Lost heart of the city,
Industrial spectres.
See, in the shimmer
Of fog drifting over,
They passed, still as evening
That falls in the cloud bank,
And leaves us no traces,
No slightest memento,
Of what we have traded
For bright, empty show.

LIII

The songs of yesteryear are like
Old sepia photographs.
The images they hold are blind
As crumbling epitaphs.
Among the growing shadows where
The lilacs arch above,
They whisper dreams but still conceal
The faces that we loved.
And voices that we think we hear
Are only sighing wind,
Across the fields of yesteryear,
Where we can't come again.
The house where we grew up is gone,
And so the loving hands.
They've overbuilt the paths we walked,
There are no open lands.
This morning early, when we stood
Beside the railroad track,
We heard the fading whispered cry
Of trains that won't come back.

LIV

Old river, you're wide and dark today,
Loud with the power of recent rain.
You fling yourself roaring against the banks,
Tearing your way through all this terrain.
You gather the soils and stain yourself brown,
And seize at the rocks and branches of trees,
Take them away with your turbulent run,
And fling them aside when they no longer please.
This power of yours is not often seen.
We walk by your banks and see you at peace.
But rain and snow melt combine to transform
Our mild old river to a foam-spotted beast.
Now give the rafters a ride to recall.
Now give the fishermen reason to doubt.
Soon enough you'll be sober and quiet again.
Today you're wild, and we hear you shout.

SNOW AND SUN

LV

Across the far-off hills,
Swirl the sibilant, white footsteps
Of the silent, sifting snow.
And the rim of my world is muffled
By the gentle, timeless silence
Of the far, white slopes
And the flat, white sky.
The sky in silence settles,
In curtaining sheets of flakes,
And softly, delicately,
Wraps everything in whiteness.

LVI

The sun scribbled on this wall today,
A mark distinct and eloquent,
Quick and crude as any graffiti,
Yet so deft the strokes
And precise the lines,
I reached to touch the paint,
Expecting to find my finger
Marked also by its vivid whiteness.
The shadow of the hand at once
Gave away the secret.
And then in swift passage,
The shining artist moved away.
Like children's chalk marks on a sidewalk,
That elusive signature faded,
Leaving the wall as bland as before.

LVII

I see the wildcat colors
In the rising of the sun.
The tiger's stripes, the leopard's spots,
Across the sky at dawn.
They lurk behind the hilltops
And pounce upon the day,
Slinking among the city's streets
And shadowed alley ways.
Descending the sides of darkened walls,
Through twilight pools they sweep,
Till in the fulfilled strength of light,
They curl up soft and sleep.

LVIII

A single clap of thunder
In darkness this morning
Announced the end
Of peaceful summer days.
Among the mountains,
Already the lightning is falling.
And bouts of rain
Scour slope and scarp
With thunderous hail.

...

There's winter, waiting,
Behind fall's brief curtain.
He'll be on stage
In just a moment,
Coursing the hilltops
Where today a rainbow shimmers
Above the last
Of summer's flowers.
We'll soon see snow.

LIX

In the red light of dawn,
And the full moon's white glow,
The roofs of the town,
The chimneys and spires,
Look like mesas and cliffs
And canyons far off.
Painted redder than life,
They are linked by that light
To wilderness vast.
For the moment untamed,
Outside of the walls,
They soar and emerge
Against the pale sky.
A brief magic it's true,
But real for that time
That the sun holds its breath,
Just beginning to climb.

LX

In the corner of the morning,
While the sun was on his way,
There was singing in the garden,
There was gleaming on the flowers,
There was light among the treetops,
And it shone through all the day.
In the corner of the noontime,
When the clouds obscured the sun,
Light was lurking in the windows,
Light was sleeping under roof beams,
Light was slipping past the darkness,
Brightening all it shone upon.
In the corner of the evening,
With the rain upon the wall,
Sunset lingered in the curtains,
Sunset flowered in the cloud-tops,
Sunset flowed across the city,
Gleaming conqueror of all.

LXI

The sky is full of violence,
The clouds clotted and grim.
Across the dull horizon,
The night is closing in.
Although the day was bright and fair,
The wind has swept away
All the calm and lovely clear,
Serene delights of day.
And now the night is facing us,
And we must bend our heads,
To wait the flailing winds and doubts
That fill the dark with dread.
Though we are surely modern folk,
No superstitious lot,
With the dark, old fears encroach,
We haven't quite forgot.
The trouble is that night-dark wind
Blows terror in its wake,
And we are none of us immune
When cold the windows shake.
We light the lamps and lock the doors,
And downward draw the shade.
The fragile refuge of our home
Becomes the barricade
Against the fears of darkness and
The violence of night,
Until the calm of daylight comes
To free us with its light.

LXII

Over there beside the morning,
Where the light of sunrise glows,
There is something we were seeking,
That the heart of silence knows.
Only in the dawnlight's coming
Can we see what darkness hid.
In the brief and passing moment,
When the works of night are led
To the auction block of waking,
Where each dream is brought to sale,
And they all must make accounting
For the ways in which they fail.
Over there beside the dawning,
Evil flees and loses form.
We will bid on what is lasting,
As we come into the morn.

LXIII

As a cat curls his tail over his toes,
So, inward curls silence at the day's close.
Little by little, seductive and warm,
It curls round our footsteps, drawing them home.
Emerging from somewhere hidden and still,
It binds all our senses with magical skill—
Inserts itself subtly, like a soft little paw,
Between us and all the clamor that draws
Attention and energy over the day,
And, almost unnoticed, waves it away.
Its powerful spell leaves us secure,
Like a cat on the lap, beginning to purr.

MOUNTAINS AND WILDERNESS

LXIV

Oh beautiful the wild, impersonal hills,
The treasury of empty places,
Golden wealth of silent canyons.
Here the dawn breaks solitary,
And tethered hearts in ceaseless dreaming
Pursue the way to dwell.
For who could but crave
Those skies deep and vast enough to hold
All the stars of the year's great circle?
Immeasurable refuge of space,
Hundred mile house on the way to Paradise,
These fierce canyons, red as the dawn,
Shelter the songs of every season,
And bar the way to all the tyrannies
And jurisdictions of despair.

LXV

The golden aspen leaves aflutter
Sing against the blue of sky.
Among the dusky greens of pine trees,
They flame like torches in the sun.
Shining largess of the autumn,
Coinage of its sovereign realm,
Freely spent in glad abundance,
Scattered with an open hand.
So they dance the wild wind's passage,
In an ecstasy of light,
Soaring, gliding, turning, swaying,
Till at last they drift to rest.
Still in undiminished splendor,
There they brighten all the earth.
In spreading pools of golden glory,
Like sunlight sleeping on the ground.

LXVI

What must it be like to live out here,
In all a wild and empty place?
Here many a long and lonely mile
Separates each from a neighbor's face.
And all of life is lived alone,
In constant silence and solitude.
Surely that is the choice men make,
Here to live. What fortitude
Makes possible that abiding place,
Alone among the rocks and hills,
Silent in all that echoing space?
The sky is always vast and cold,
With no regard for mortal man,
And little refuge grant the rocks.
Let him abide there, he who can.
We who pass along the road
Have little sense of what we see.
A sign that reads Ranch Exit, yes.
But can we guess what that might be?
Ranch Exit from the cares of life?
Ah, no, the cares come home with you,
Whether you leave the road right there,
Or ride its miles the whole way through.

LXVII

The wind roars always in this place.
Unceasingly, it cries.
What are the burdens that it mourns,
The fears from which it flies?
For like some weary, haggard crone,
It wanders through the land,
Casting the dust upon its head,
Weeping behind its hand.
And ever as the morning comes,
You see its footsteps near.
The evening too aligns its pace.
At night its woe you hear.
Oh, wind, let sorrow fade away,
And rest yourself at last.
We too would find relief to see
That all your grief was past.

LXVIII

Oh, purple mountain majesties,
How bored you must become
With foolish wealthy folk who think
To rule in your kingdom.
Among the solemn canyons and
The peaks they'll never know,
The ancient hidden pathways where
Only the silence goes.
Don't you wish they'd hurry up
And tire of this pretense,
For they'll be always limited
To places they can fence.
And when their time has come and gone,
Like miners without gold,
Your undiminished glory still
Its secrets will withhold.

PARABLES AND VISIONS

LXIX

Like barnacles,
Like monkey's claws,
Things cling to one,
Hampering all movement.
Each gesture toward change
Awakens bitter cries of despair,
Cruel hurt, abandonment, betrayal.
Ever heavier they weigh,
Children grown too large to be carried,
Yet clinging, pleading, as if for life itself.
Their stony weight refuses to grant
The freedom of gladness—
Unencumbered arms and breath
For running headlong up the hill.
The journey will continue all the same;
We know the caravan master's voice.
But turning to the trek,
For long we'll walk, nursing the ragged gaps
Those clinging claws have torn.

LXX

ARCHÆOLOGY

Our days are shattered like the shards
Of some forgotten ancient pot,
And pieced together by the hands
Of modern folk who know them not.
They can't remember time or place,
Or see the use or tell the grace
Of what was made to hold the wine
Or joy the heart of another time.
They take the pieces that remain,
Though lost the heart of the design,
And fit together what will show
They understand the shape and line.
What pots are meant to be, they know,
And certain of the way to go,
The thing they now will shape anew
Must learn another task to do.
Its form the function will reflect
The only thing they see it as,
Its place among the well-known facts,
The only test it has to pass.
And in the end, the form alone,
Corroded now, an ancient bone,
Stands there on some museum shelf,
A mere extension of itself.
They'll stand around to gaze and say,
Techniques were poor; they did not know
The potter's wheel technology
To make pots uniform and so—

It's primitive and poorly made.
And all the arguments arrayed
Could never hope to make them see
The shape as it was meant to be.
For pieces missing made the line.
Without them, lost is the design.
We think we know, and all along,
We know indeed, but know it wrong.

LXXI

Time and change cannot erase
The morning from long years ago.
Wakened suddenly to face
A challenge that I could not know.
Nor could I stop the tragedy
That made a heroine that day,
Our mother cat who would not flee,
Though terror took her life away.
The dogs came in the dark, you see,
To seize the kittens that she bore,
And she, to save her family,
Fought till she could fight no more.
Where she fell, she, dying, lay.
With heavy heart I brought her home,
Knowing she could never stay,
And in the sunrise, she was gone.
The kittens that she died to spare
Could not live, left so alone.
Their tiny lives, despite our care,
Could not make it on their own.
Her death was wasted, you may say.
The enemy was beaten though.
Her kittens died a gentler way.
She was the victor, even so.
For after all these years are gone,
Her gallant sacrifice preserves
The truth that faithfulness is one
With glory such a strength deserves.
The enemies are ever near,
In cruel hatred to attack.
Against their ill our way is clear,
At any cost to drive them back.

LXXII

Love has the color of morning,
A hue too subtle to name,
Though its elements gleam in the sunrise,
The glory of daylight,
Surrounding the clouds with its flame.
Love has the color of midnight,
Deeper than blue of the sea,
Darker than starlight and shadows,
Cast on black boulders,
Enshrouding profound mystery.
Love has the color of rainfall,
Transparent till filled with the sun,
Then gleaming in colors too vibrant
For open-eyed viewing,
Or unshuttered gazing upon.
Love has the color of starlight,
So softly it reaches our eyes,
Though shot through with glitter and glory,
It slips past defenses,
And takes the glad heart by surprise.

LXXIII

Gale eight is blowing now along
The corridors of what we know.
It sweeps the changing years away,
Carries before it every show
Of pride and dream and destiny.
Down from the mountains swooping wild,
Its power invades the palisades.
There is no rampart strong enough
To hold against its flying raids
Or shelter anything for trade.
We do not know the demon's name,
To call a halt, to bid it stay.
Before the blast we cry in vain.
It carries all our spells away
And leaves us lorn to face the day.

LXXIV

The pythia upon her stool,
Don't you wonder what she saw?
The sights her words could not convey,
For which they called her double-tongued.
She drank the vapor willingly
To hear the voice of God,
And see what mortals cannot perceive.
How could her ears contain that Voice?
How could her eyes look
And afterward still see?
I think the pythias all died young.
For flames that bright can't burn for long.
And where they walked in ecstasy
Is far too steep a path
For any human foot not washed
In those bright waters, pure and cold,
That flow through the City of God.

LXXV

Old fields of memory,
What crops do you grow,
Now that the farmers
No longer come home?
Where are the harvests
Your acres could yield,
Now that no tiller
Is tending your field?
Nettles and briers
Encroach on your rows.
Sorrow and silence
Year by year grows.
Furrows left fallow
Encourage but weeds.
There can be no harvest
Where there are no seeds.
Here is the witness
Whose voice must prevail,
That all of creation now
Groans in travail.

LXXVI

I hid a butterfly here, she said,
A little girl, at play in the park.
She'd never guess the pure delight
It gave to one who heard her remark.
An instant vision of magical scenes
Transformed the drab park to a fairyland,
Where butterflies play hide and seek,
And wonder awaits the trusting hand.
Where magic rewards the willing search,
The confident heart that, unafraid,
Looks past the dullness that limits us
And reaches to touch the dream it made.
Bright visions last but a little while.
But when the shadows darken the sky,
That trusting childhood voice recalls,
Right here we hid a butterfly.

LXXVII

Sitting back here in the shadows,
It's just silhouettes that I see.
The details of faces and figures
Are obscure and hidden to me.
Lips may curve gently in laughter,
Eyes may be full of delight.
But I am back here in the shadows,
And backlight obscures from my sight,
Reducing the forms to an image,
Like black basalt statues that may,
Lighted by favors of sunlight,
Show all of the form they portray.
More often the darkness obscures them.
Expression and person are lost.
And only the stone's heavy darkness
From their time to our time has crossed.

LXXVIII

Just for a fleeting instant,
I thought I saw it clear.
Freed from limits of blindness,
But tinged with an aura of fear.
Vision is not for the timid,
Not fully committed heart.
For though it comes with glory,
There is also a fearful part.
Its power demands surrender.
Its way is downward through change,
Shadows of loss and renewal,
Before we reach its high range.
Visions are lovely in looking,
But hard with the color of fear.
In the brief instant of seeing,
Note well the paradox here.
Hidden there in the grasses,
Bound with ecstatic dread,
Like a gleaming snake or a flower,
It rears its beautiful head.

LXXIX

That leopard skin the priest of old
Used to wear so proud and bold,
At last became a heavy load.
The spotted fur that should have borne
Its wearer through his forest home,
Grew heavy as a granite stone.
Those dangling claws across his chest
That would have served the leopard best,
In time deprived the land of rest.
The empty eyes that stared amazed
Between the old priest's shoulder blades,
Became the scales in which were weighed
The sum and total of their ways.
When judged, they found no coin to pay
For what one leopard skin would weigh.

BEASTS AND BIRDS

LXXX

Snow Leopards in a Zoo

With eyes like silence, they,
Lying along the gray, unfeatured line
Of what was once a tree,
Regard my passage—
One with countless others in their days.
Unexceptional for them the gaze
I turn upon their famous, spotted heads.
They will not shift their own gaze
To see me come or go.
For they are still,
Dwelling within a cool suspension,
Their being split off by the moment of capture.
The life they know, they cannot lead;
The life they lead, they cannot know.
And so—
They see their own sights past me,
Only another bar on the cage,
No longer possible to notice.
And I, in silence centered,
As in the gaze of their golden eyes,
Have left unspoken the words I carried here,
To praise their beauty.

LXXXI

Among the portraits in the album,
This one stands out.
The lions lie in pride formation,
Elaborately unconcealed.
Here are the patriarchs,
All golden manes and languid paws.
Their calm, faintly supercilious great-cat faces
In perfect poses of dominance.
Six lionesses, deceptively somnolent,
Watch with slitted amber eyes.
One curls a paw
And bends her head to wash.
But ears flick back and forth,
So nothing passes by unseen.
A scatter of cubs
Rolls and runs, like children everywhere.
They mimic their elders in battle and hunt.
Sunlight casts a glamour over them all.
You cannot see the ribs hurting with hunger,
The broken tooth, the limping foot.
Their history secure, their future more uncertain,
Happy creatures of innocent arrogance,
They live fearless of shadows they cannot see.

LXXXII

She sits there,
Sometimes on the deck,
Sometimes on the fence.
A dove, small and gray and alone.
Her smooth, round head tucked in,
She huddles, even in sunlight's warmth.
So still she waits.
Her well-known mourning cry
Is heard no more.
Yet to the watching eye, she seems
All clad in widow's weeds.
Her tearful voice is still,
But all her stooped form weeps.
They mate for life, it's said, and she
Somewhere has lost her life.
Solitary, silent she sits,
Until, solitary, uncomprehending, she flies.

LXXXIII

The hawks are calling in the sky,
Like the kites' wild, ceaseless keening.
Old Egypt glorified their cry
As bereft goddesses' deep mourning.
Here the crows, with raucous laughter,
Crudely mock their loss and sorrow.
Yet, their crying does not falter.
With each high wail, its powers grow.
Grief is like that, overwhelming.
Its tears drown every other voice.
While it lasts, it's all-consuming.
Where it stands, none can rejoice.

LXXXIV

The tiger, by the forest's edge,
Was looking for the way,
And sat down there in weariness,
Toward the end of day.
And looking to the darkening sky,
He saw the evening star,
And there beside it in the west,
The full moon shining clear.
With light like this, the way must be
Clearly seen and known.
And so the tiger rose and turned,
To see the pathway home.
But in the gloom of forest glade,
The moon and stars were hid,
And nowhere could the eye discern
The way the trails led.
And there the tiger must remain,
With all the sky aglow.
Because the earth in shadow lies,
There is no light below.
Tomorrow when the daylight comes,
With all the power of sun,
It's only then the tiger's eye
Will find his pathway home.

LXXXV

I had to stand here,
The old leopard said.
This was the place that needed me.
I had to wait here,
Till the morning
Sets the fettered forest free.
See, it isn't mine to hunt them,
Till the chains are loosed again,
And the prey and predator
Can resume their bond of kin.
It is only foolish fancy
To imagine we can go
While the world is bound around us,
While our way we cannot know.
I will have to wait yet longer,
Said the leopard patiently,
Until all the chains of sorrow
Have been loosed, and we are free.

INDEX OF TITLES AND FIRST LINES

The tiger, by the forest's edge, 117

The wind roars always in this place, 94

There is no one now to carry us in, 14

They're naming the county roads now, 38

This morning's sun, with precise beam, 61

Those silly pigeons, 63

Through the open door, the sunlight slants, 30

Time and change cannot erase, 102

To walk down along that road again, 40

Today there is a man by the door, 7

Walking in the wind, I am reminded, 12

Walking through the streets, 21

Wandering from room to room, 67

What must it be like to live out here, 93

Where was I when there was spoken, 50

While down the street in solitude, 58

Who lives in these houses, whose bright, lighted windows, 23

Will they ask us at the gateway, 48

With eyes like silence, they, 113

ABOUT THE AUTHOR

LEANNA GASKINS spent her early years on a Kansas wheat farm without electricity, gas, or inside plumbing. She went to school in Dodge City and then to the University of Kansas, transferring when invited to a program in economics at Rampart College, in the mountains of Colorado.

She moved to Los Angeles where she spent several years and married. She graduated as a Regents Scholar from the University of California, Berkeley, and earned a Ph.D. in Linguistics there, applying modern formal linguistic theory to the ancient Egyptian language written in hieroglyphic, which she also taught to a generation of UC Berkeley Egyptology students.

Anticipating the coming importance of personal computers, she moved to Silicon Valley to join very early startup software companies as a teacher, writer, and manager of writing groups. During this same period she researched railroad history in travels over all the western states, and was one of a small team who rebuilt and restored the long-dormant Southern Pacific 2472 steam locomotive.

She retired very early and moved with her husband to central London where they lived and studied for ten years, after which they returned to live in San Francisco. She has written poetry since her early college years.

www.ingramcontent.com/pod-product-compliance
Lightning Source LLC
LaVergne TN
LVHW091224080426
835509LV00009B/1148